SOPHOCLES

Sophocles (c. 496–405 BC) was an ancient Greek tragedian. Of his more than 120 plays, only seven have survived in a complete form: *Ajax*, *Antigone*, *Women of Trachis*, *Oedipus Rex*, *Electra*, *Philoctetes* and *Oedipus at Colonus*.

ELLA HICKSON

Ella Hickson is an award-winning writer whose work has been performed throughout the UK and abroad. Her plays include *Adult Children*, a 2022 VR collaboration between Donmar Warehouse, ETT and Trial and Error Studio; *Swive [Elizabeth]*, which opened at the Sam Wanamaker Playhouse at Shakespeare's Globe in 2019; and *ANNA*, created with Ben and Max Ringham, which opened at the National Theatre in 2019. *The Writer* and *Oil* opened at the Almeida Theatre in 2018 and 2017 respectively. In 2013–15 *Wendy & Peter Pan*, adapted from the book by J.M. Barrie, played to wide acclaim at the Royal Shakespeare Company. Other credits include *Riot Girls* (Radio 4); *Boys* (Nuffield Theatre Southampton/Headlong Theatre/HighTide Festival Theatre); *Decade* (Headlong Theatre/St Katharine Docks); *The Authorised Kate Bane* (Grid Iron/Traverse Theatre, Edinburgh); *Rightfully Mine* (Radio 4); *Precious Little Talent* (Trafalgar Studios/Tantrums Productions); *Hot Mess* (Arcola Tent/Tantrums Productions) and *Eight* (Trafalgar Studios/Bedlam Theatre, Edinburgh). She is a member of the Royal Society of Literature, a MacDowell and Yaddo Fellow and recipient of The Catherine Johnson Award. She is developing new work with the Donmar Warehouse, the RSC, The Berliner Ensemble, Sonia Friedman Productions and ATG.

Other Titles in this Series

Waleed Akhtar
THE ART OF ILLUSION *after* Alexis Michalik
KABUL GOES POP: MUSIC TELEVISION
    AFGHANISTAN
THE P WORD
THE REAL ONES

Jez Butterworth
THE FERRYMAN
THE HILLS OF CALIFORNIA
JERUSALEM
JEZ BUTTERWORTH PLAYS: ONE
JEZ BUTTERWORTH PLAYS: TWO
MOJO
THE NIGHT HERON
PARLOUR SONG
THE RIVER
THE WINTERLING

Caryl Churchill
BLUE HEART
CHURCHILL PLAYS: THREE
CHURCHILL PLAYS: FOUR
CHURCHILL PLAYS: FIVE
CHURCHILL: SHORTS
CLOUD NINE
DING DONG THE WICKED
A DREAM PLAY *after* Strindberg
DRUNK ENOUGH TO SAY I LOVE YOU?
ESCAPED ALONE
FAR AWAY
GLASS. KILL. BLUEBEARD'S FRIENDS.
    IMP.
HERE WE GO
HOTEL
ICECREAM
LIGHT SHINING IN BUCKINGHAMSHIRE
LOVE AND INFORMATION
MAD FOREST
A NUMBER
PIGS AND DOGS
SEVEN JEWISH CHILDREN
THE SKRIKER
THIS IS A CHAIR
THYESTES *after* Seneca
TRAPS
WHAT IF IF ONLY

Natasha Gordon
NINE NIGHT

Ella Hickson
ANNA
THE AUTHORISED KATE BANE
BOYS
EIGHT
OIL
PRECIOUS LITTLE TALENT & HOT MESS
SWIVE [ELIZABETH]
WENDY & PETER PAN *after* J.M. Barrie
THE WRITER

Rhianna Ilube
SAMUEL TAKES A BREAK… IN MALE
    DUNGEON NO. 5 AFTER A LONG
    BUT GENERALLY SUCCESSFUL
    DAY OF TOURS

Branden Jacobs-Jenkins
APPROPRIATE
THE COMEUPPANCE
GLORIA
AN OCTOROON

Lucy Kirkwood
BEAUTY AND THE BEAST
    with Katie Mitchell
BLOODY WIMMIN
THE CHILDREN
CHIMERICA
HEDDA *after* Ibsen
THE HUMAN BODY
IT FELT EMPTY WHEN THE HEART
    WENT AT FIRST BUT IT IS
    ALRIGHT NOW
LUCY KIRKWOOD PLAYS: ONE
MOSQUITOES
NSFW
RAPTURE
TINDERBOX
THE WELKIN

Benedict Lombe
LAVA
SHIFTERS

Winsome Pinnock
LEAVE TAKING
ROCKETS AND BLUE LIGHTS
TAKEN
TITUBA

Mark Rosenblatt
GIANT

Jack Thorne
2ND MAY 1997
AFTER LIFE
BUNNY
BURYING YOUR BROTHER IN
    THE PAVEMENT
A CHRISTMAS CAROL *after* Dickens
THE END OF HISTORY…
HOPE
JACK THORNE PLAYS: ONE
JACK THORNE PLAYS: TWO
JUNKYARD
LET THE RIGHT ONE IN
    after John Ajvide Lindqvist
THE MOTIVE AND THE CUE
MYDIDAE
THE SOLID LIFE OF SUGAR WATER
STACY & FANNY AND FAGGOT
WHEN WINSTON WENT TO WAR WITH
    THE WIRELESS
WHEN YOU CURE ME
WOYZECK *after* Büchner

debbie tucker green
BORN BAD
DEBBIE TUCKER GREEN PLAYS: ONE
DIRTY BUTTERFLY
EAR FOR EYE
HANG
NUT
A PROFOUNDLY AFFECTIONATE,
    PASSIONATE DEVOTION TO
    SOMEONE (– *NOUN*)
RANDOM
STONING MARY
TRADE & GENERATIONS
TRUTH AND RECONCILIATION

Ross Willis
WOLFIE
WONDER BOY

Sophocles

OEDIPUS

in a version by
Ella Hickson

NICK HERN BOOKS
London
www.nickhernbooks.co.uk

A Nick Hern Book

This version of *Oedipus* first published as a paperback original in Great Britain in 2025 by Nick Hern Books Limited, The Glasshouse, 49a Goldhawk Road, London W12 8QP

This version of *Oedipus* © 2025 Ella Hickson

Ella Hickson has asserted her right to be identified as the author of this work

Cover: photograph of Rami Malek and Indira Varma by Nadav Kande

Designed and typeset by Nick Hern Books, London
Printed in Great Britain by Mimeo Ltd, Huntingdon, Cambridgeshire PE29 6XX

A CIP catalogue record for this book is available from the British Library

ISBN 978 1 83904 410 6

CAUTION All rights whatsoever in this play are strictly reserved. Requests to reproduce the text in whole or in part should be addressed to the publisher.

Amateur Performing Rights Applications for performance, including readings and excerpts, by amateurs in the English language throughout the world should be addressed to the Performing Rights Manager, Nick Hern Books, The Glasshouse, 49a Goldhawk Road, London W12 8QP, *tel* +44 (0)20 8749 4953, *email* rights@nickhernbooks.co.uk, except as follows:

Australia: ORiGiN Theatrical, *email* enquiries@originmusic.com.au, *web* www.origintheatrical.com.au

New Zealand: Play Bureau, 20 Rua Street, Mangapapa, Gisborne, 4010, *tel* +64 21 258 3998, *email* info@playbureau.com

USA and Canada: Casarotto Ramsay and Associates Ltd, see details below

Professional Performing Rights Applications for performance by professionals in any medium and in any language throughout the world (including by stock companies in the USA and Canada) should be addressed to Casarotto Ramsay and Associates Ltd, *email* rights@casarotto.co.uk, www.casarotto.co.uk

No performance of any kind may be given unless a licence has been obtained. Applications should be made before rehearsals begin. Publication of this play does not necessarily indicate its availability for amateur performance.

www.nickhernbooks.co.uk/environmental-policy

Nick Hern Books' authorised representative in the EU is
Easy Access System Europe – Mustamäe tee 50, 10621 Tallinn, Estonia
email gpsr.requests@easproject.com

This version of *Oedipus* was first performed at The Old Vic, London, on 21 January 2025, as an Old Vic Production in association with Hofesh Shechter Company. The cast was as follows:

OEDIPUS	Rami Malek
JOCASTA	Indira Varma
CREON	Nicholas Khan
CORINTHIAN	Joseph Mydell
TIRESIAS	Cecilia Noble
SHEPHERD	Nicholas Woodeson

CHILDREN

ANTIGONE	Róisín Bhalla, Amandeep Panesar, Asha Thakrar
ISMENE	Annika Chugh, Rosa Neill-Chetty, Amelia Valentina Pankhania

DANCERS

Justine Gouache, Charles Heinrich, Kenny Wing Tao Ho, Adam Khazhmuradov, Kim Kohlmann, Oscar Jinghu Li, Yen-Ching Lin, Rachelle Scott, Jian-Hui Wang, Zee Zunnur

UNDERSTUDIES

OEDIPUS/CREON	Fayez Bakhsh
CORINTHIAN/SHEPHERD	Paul Easom
JOCASTA/TIRESIAS	Sarah Priddy

Co-Director, Choreographer & Music	Hofesh Shechter
Co-Director	Matthew Warchus
Set & Costume	Rae Smith
Lighting	Tom Visser
Sound	Christopher Shutt
Casting	Jim Carnahan, CSA
Children's Casting	Saffeya Shebli
Voice	Charlie Hughes-D'Aeth
Dialect	Penny Dyer
Fights	Terry King
Associate Director	Lilac Yosiphon
Associate Choreographer	Kim Kohlmann
Associate Set	Niall McKeever
Associate Costume	Joanna Coe
Associate Lighting	Chris Burr
Music Collaborator	Frédéric Despierre
Props Supervisor	Propworks
Wigs, Hair & Make-Up Supervisor	Campbell Young Associates
Company Manager	Tamsin Withers
Stage Manager	Graham Michael
Deputy Stage Manager	Maria Gibbons
Assistant Stage Manager (Book Cover)	Shakira Taylor-Knight

Acknowledgements

My thanks to Matthew Warchus, Maria Gibbons, Lilac Yosiphon, the brilliant cast, Harriet Mackie, the Vermont Studio Centre, the Hawthornden Foundation, Rachel Taylor, Amy Rosenthal and, of course, Omer and Noa Bor.

E.H.

'The future isn't what it used to be'

Alan Parker, Angel Heart

Characters

OEDIPUS
CREON
JOCASTA
ANTIGONE
ISMENE
TIRESIAS
CORINTHIAN
SHEPHERD
THE ELDERS
THE PEOPLE

This text went to press before the end of rehearsals and so may differ slightly from the play as performed.

Place – Thebes – 2520

Sun: there is nothing. Dirt and arid desert; hard, cracked ground. An unforgiving sun sits low in the sky giving perpetual, scorching heat. Even at night, there is no relief.

Dance

Scene One

The middle of the night – the Palace of Thebes.

OEDIPUS *stands alone – he waits, impatiently.*

CREON *enters.*

–

OEDIPUS. You took your time.

CREON. I was at the gates, amongst the people, they've brought their dead with them.

OEDIPUS. Okay.

CREON. There are priests burning incense. They've seen bird omens over the palace.

OEDIPUS. I've decided to release our private store of water. Give it to the people, don't tell them it's the last.

CREON. I'm not sure /

OEDIPUS. / You're objecting to sharing the royal store with the people?

CREON. I'm not sure releasing more water is the answer. I've been at the gates /

OEDIPUS. / You said.

CREON. They're praying.

OEDIPUS. For water, so go and answer their prayers.

CREON. We want you to pray with us. Only the Gods can offer real salvation.

JOCASTA *enters*.

JOCASTA. Oedipus, the girls are asking for you.

OEDIPUS (*to* JOCASTA). I'll be right there. (*To* CREON.) Go tell the people they're getting more water.

CREON. What they want is your prayer.

JOCASTA. Not more than water, surely?

CREON. It's a danger to ignore people who feel so strongly.

JOCASTA. Danger, how?

CREON. Oedipus, their faith... our faith, is a fire.

JOCASTA. You think you're the only one coming, tap tap tap, on this door?

OEDIPUS. The girls, I don't want them to be alone.

JOCASTA, *reluctantly, leaves*.

CREON. A man of faith, is a man of strength. My faction follows me without question.

OEDIPUS (*smiles*). Yes, Creon – but not everyone is looking to be followed without question. Your robe is slightly askew.

OEDIPUS *rearranges his robe for him*.

Is there anything else?

CREON. Twenty years ago, the last time the land was dry, you allowed the Gods to speak through you, you defeated the Sphinx and the rains came. The people were saved. If you open to faith once again /

OEDIPUS. / You're in good hands, all of you. Trust me.

CREON *bows, exits*.

JOCASTA *enters*.

JOCASTA. The girls are sleeping, for now.

OEDIPUS. Good.

JOCASTA. Does my brother think seeing a king get down on his knees and raise his hands to the sky is what people need when they're starving?

OEDIPUS. It's what some people need, maybe.

JOCASTA. His priests are leaving half-burnt animals rotting in the riverbed, they're encouraging women to breed when the city can't feed the children it already has.

OEDIPUS. Babies are hopeful.

JOCASTA. There's a limit to hope and that limit is reality. Come to bed, you need to rest.

OEDIPUS. I need to keep them on side.

JOCASTA. Why?

OEDIPUS. It's time to go.

JOCASTA. Leave Thebes?

OEDIPUS. We'll have to leave the sick behind. We'll need the young and healthy most of all, and a lot of them are in Creon's faction. They've been up for days, chanting, singing – no water, no food and they're still going. They're strong. Something's fuelling them.

JOCASTA. Something like what?

OEDIPUS. We need them with us.

JOCASTA. They won't leave Thebes. The city is built on a sacred site.

OEDIPUS. They might leave.

JOCASTA. How?

OEDIPUS. If I consult an Oracle.

JOCASTA. –

OEDIPUS. It shows humility – and – whatever the Oracle says…

JOCASTA. –

OEDIPUS. Like I did with the Sphinx – I answered the riddle with my mind, they think I'm divinely inspired. Whatever the Oracle gives us, it'll be an abstract thing, it's never so specific. I can work with it. If we're going to find water, if we're going to survive, I need the faithful with us.

JOCASTA. A woman this afternoon sacrificed her eldest child to the Gods, believing it would save the other two.

OEDIPUS. –

JOCASTA. That woman will have killed her child and then what? Stared at the sky, put her bloody hands out, waited for the rain to start – and nothing. Then looked back at her child's body on the dry, dry ground. (*Beat*.) Where are you at, as a leader, once you've sanctioned that sort of thing? It's barbaric.

OEDIPUS. I think they think our pragmatism, in these circumstances, is barbaric. They think it's hubris – not to ask the Gods for help.

JOCASTA. What if what we need to do now, is not fix or solve – there's no water, there may be no water – what if, what we need to do, as leaders, is to face the end of things, bravely – and we show them how to do that.

OEDIPUS *rubs her shoulders, kisses her, appeases her*.

OEDIPUS. I know what I'm doing.

I know what I'm doing.

She kisses him.

JOCASTA. Don't consult the Oracle. They're evil. It's the one thing I'm asking you not to do.

OEDIPUS. You're sounding sort of religious about it.

OEDIPUS *kisses her*.

–

A VOICE (*from the shadows*). Daddy?

They break apart.

JOCASTA. Antigone.

> JOCASTA *puts her arms out for* ANTIGONE. OEDIPUS *gets there first and grabs his kid. He tickles her, squeezes her, tries to play a game.* ANTIGONE *laughs, then stops.*

ANTIGONE. It's too hot to sleep. Ismene keeps making noises.

JOCASTA. Come here, bubba. Let me tell you a story.

ANTIGONE. Is there any water?

Pause.

OEDIPUS. I'll find you some.

ANTIGONE. Really?

OEDIPUS. Yes, really.

> OEDIPUS *laughs, squeezes his kid.* ANTIGONE *laughs.* JOCASTA *looks on, concerned.*

ANTIGONE. Can I have the water now?

JOCASTA. Antigone, come.

> JOCASTA *exits – thinking* ANTIGONE *will follow her,* ANTIGONE *runs back to* OEDIPUS.

ANTIGONE. Daddy? Are you scared?

OEDIPUS. Daddies don't get scared. Come here.

He hugs her.

I love you.

ANTIGONE *goes inside.* OEDIPUS *stares – devastated.*

OEDIPUS *looks in the direction that* CREON *went. He exits.*

Dance

Scene Two

OEDIPUS *and* JOCASTA, *with* ANTIGONE *and* ISMENE, *walk out to address* THE PEOPLE.

OEDIPUS. People of Thebes, our people, we see your suffering. We feel your pain as if it was from within our own family. We share your grief over the devastation of our proud and beautiful land, our city aches. The royal family is happy to share our water reserves, meagre though they are. I hope this will bring us some small relief.

THE ELDERS. Will you consult with the Gods?

OEDIPUS. I have a plan that will act on our common hope to see our people thrive.

Discord and discontent from THE PEOPLE.

I arrived at your city gates, an outsider, twenty years ago – and you welcomed me. When I defeated the Sphinx –

THE ELDERS. Guided by the Gods.

OEDIPUS. You elected me as your leader. An honour that I have tried to meet. I have come to know you well. Those of you who were my age when I arrived, I speak to you now as my brothers and sisters. We have grown together, become masters of our work, married, become parents, leaders of this city. We're starting to grey a little, huh? But in a good way, I think. (*Shoots them a grin.*) Those of you older than me, I speak as your son, full of love, respect and gratitude for the counsel you have offered me over the years. Counsel that has allowed me to govern well.

To those of you whom I have seen rise, alongside my own children, from newborns, like the dawn sun, into strong and smiling youths, full of hope and inventive light – I speak to you now as a father, astounded by your resilience in these times, times that no child should have to face.

When I arrived, you gifted me the opportunity to be your leader, and I promised to lead you with courage, conviction and ingenuity. Now, now is the time that I come good on that promise. People of Thebes, in the name of our ancestors, for the sake of our children – we must leave this city. Follow me towards the boundary of what we believe is possible. There is opportunity beyond these walls and together, we will reach for it! Using Theban resolve and determination, we will go as one in search of new and flourishing lands.

THE ELDERS. The city is built on a sacred site.

We cannot afford to anger the Gods any more than we already have. Leaving the city will guarantee our destruction.

JOCASTA. Staying in the city will guarantee our destruction.

THE ELDERS. The Gods will guide us.

Why would you not offer your piety when the welfare of your people relies on it?

Turmoil from THE PEOPLE.

JOCASTA. The welfare of the people relies on water, leaving Thebes is the only chance we have of finding...

The noise of THE PEOPLE *overwhelms her.* OEDIPUS *quietens them.*

OEDIPUS. Late last night, I stood alone at the city boundary and looked... miles of dry earth surround us on every side. This city was founded with an altar. The faithful have guided us ever since. I sent Prince Creon into the desert to consult the Oracle.

THE PEOPLE *erupt, there is great hope and relief.*

JOCASTA. Oedipus?

OEDIPUS. It's alright.

CREON *enters carrying an ancient container – oblong – it is both old and new.*

JOCASTA (*aside*). Oedipus.

OEDIPUS (*aside*). It's alright – I'll handle it.

CREON. Sister.

> CREON *places the large case on a table.* CREON *opens the box, revealing a reel-to-reel machine. He lifts it up, presents it to* THE PEOPLE; *the metal glints, the tape is taut and shining.*
>
> OEDIPUS *approaches the* ORACLE. THE PEOPLE *rejoice.*
>
> CREON *raises* OEDIPUS*'s hand high.* THE PEOPLE *bask in the confidence.*
>
> King Oedipus, who saved us when he defeated the Sphinx! King Oedipus, in his great wisdom, has turned to the Gods. King Oedipus will save us once again!
>
> –
>
> OEDIPUS *approaches the* ORACLE – *he presses play.*
>
> *The machine whirrs to life.*

ORACLE. YOU SUFFER BECAUSE THERE HAS BEEN A CONTAMINATION OF THIS LAND. THE GODS COMMAND THAT THE LAND IS PURIFIED. THE CONTAMINATION HAS BEEN ALLOWED TO THRIVE BECAUSE YOU HAVE IGNORED IT. ALLOWING THIS CONTAMINATION TO THRIVE HAS MADE IT INCURABLE.

> *The machine stops –* OEDIPUS *stares at the machine, waiting for more… Silence.*

OEDIPUS (*to* THE PEOPLE). There has been a contamination of this land. The contamination is incurable so we must leave and find new land.

CREON. The Gods command that this land is purified.

OEDIPUS. We have no water for purification. So, we must leave.

CREON. We can purify by banishment or slaughter; we can purify this land with blood.

OEDIPUS. Mm.

JOCASTA. Blood?

THE PEOPLE *react positively to* CREON*'s idea.*

OEDIPUS *takes* CREON *to one side.*

CREON. It's man that suffers, so it's man that must have sinned. So, it's man that must be punished. The people, my people –

OEDIPUS. Your people?

CREON. The People of God. My King, we all understand that this much suffering...

He looks out at THE PEOPLE.

...is a punishment. We wish to take responsibility for our wrongdoing.

JOCASTA. You want to kill more people than are already dying?

OEDIPUS. People of Thebes, be ready at dawn, we are leaving this city.

The ORACLE *bursts to life of its own accord* –

ORACLE. KING LAIUS RULED THIS LAND BEFORE KING OEDIPUS. HE WAS MURDERED, AND HIS MURDERERS WERE NEVER PUNISHED. THE PERPETRATORS OF THIS CRIME MUST BE FOUND AND PUNISHED. THEN THE LAND SHALL BE CLEAN AND THE RAINS WILL COME.

THE PEOPLE *go silent.*

CREON (*zealous*). The murder of King Laius.

CREON *grabs* OEDIPUS *in joy.*

We are blessed to know it, to be reminded, it is our failing that we... (*To* JOCASTA.) Your husband's murder went unavenged. (*To* OEDIPUS.) We were so excited by you

solving the Sphinx that we never – of course. (*To* THE
PEOPLE.) We are blessed. We have received guidance,
salvation, deliverance – the Gods have spoken!

CREON *raises his hands to the sky, clasps* OEDIPUS *in a hug.*

JOCASTA. How can Laius's murder, so long ago, cause a drought?

CREON. Neglect can cause a tree to die. Selfishness can be the cause of a poisoned river. Ignorance can cause the death of a herd, so, of course, sin can cause drought.

THE PEOPLE *voice their affirmations throughout this section.*

JOCASTA. You're mixing morality and nature.

OEDIPUS. Jocasta.

CREON. The Gods have given us cause and cure.

JOCASTA. We need to leave. It's our only option.

CREON. King Laius's murder must be avenged.

THE ELDERS. Then the rains will come, then the People of Thebes will be healed. King Oedipus will save his people once again.

–

OEDIPUS *watches* THE PEOPLE; *he is moved by them –* CREON *steps back and indicates for* OEDIPUS *to speak.* OEDIPUS *takes a beat – looks at them… proceeds.*

–

OEDIPUS. King Laius's murderers will be found. His murder will be avenged. The rains will come, and the People of Thebes will be healed.

THE PEOPLE *move,* OEDIPUS *is drawn to it.*

If anyone has any information about the death of King Laius, you should come forward with it now. If anyone in this city is guilty and is staying silent through fear or is trying to protect someone they love, be certain – be *certain*, that you will be caught. I am unflinching in my ambition – I will find and punish the men who took King Laius's life from him. I will show no mercy and this land, our land, will be saved.

THE PEOPLE *go wild* – OEDIPUS *stares*. CREON *takes one of* OEDIPUS*'s hands – they drink it in.*

CREON. Thank you. Bless you and thank you. Our great leader.

OEDIPUS. Light your incense... take your children in your arms, tell them that King Oedipus will end their suffering.

Dance

Scene Three

Inside the Palace.

JOCASTA *stands, broods*. OEDIPUS *enters – he sees her, stops – they stare.*

JOCASTA. Are you feeling better? Relaxed? The death of King Laius, of course. Silly of me not to think of it myself. Of course that's what has caused the drought, not years of leeching off the land.

OEDIPUS. Were there any witnesses?

JOCASTA. How are you going to get everyone on the road now you've got an historic murder investigation to solve?

OEDIPUS. It's okay. It won't take long.

JOCASTA. It was twenty years ago.

OEDIPUS. We'll get it done, and then we'll go.

JOCASTA. They're crazies, wackos.

OEDIPUS. I need everyone together.

JOCASTA. Together? Well – one of the servants is already accusing a cousin she hates; that cousin is blaming the guy he thinks is fucking his wife, says he's going to save the city by killing him. And what about the others who aren't out there with their hands in the air? They think their leader has lost his mind.

OEDIPUS. Have you finished?

JOCASTA. Maybe you'd be delighted for our salvation to be in the hands of the Gods; it would give you a break.

OEDIPUS. When have I ever done anything but take total responsibility for myself, my decisions, this family and the citizens of Thebes? I'm giving us and our children a shot at salvation.

JOCASTA. There are people who have had to sit and watch their loved ones die – that is the hardest work of anyone's life, to give the dying peace… and now you have riled zealots with sticks who are going to hunt and catch and kick and kill – in the name of the Gods. The cowardice is unforgivable!

OEDIPUS. You think the death of a king shouldn't be avenged? You think it's okay that he was murdered, and his murderers went free? He was your husband.

JOCASTA. That is a whole other conversation.

OEDIPUS. Well I hope I don't get offed on a dark night and everyone just forgets about it.

JOCASTA. He was murdered by robbers. They weren't from here; they fled the scene.

OEDIPUS. Who reported that to you? That they were robbers, and they fled?

JOCASTA. I want you to say to my face that children are dying of thirst because we didn't find Laius's murderers.

OEDIPUS. Who reported it to you?

JOCASTA. 'Children are dying of thirst because we didn't find Laius's murderers.'

OEDIPUS. Who witnessed the crime?!

Every king in history has been backed by God, it's only us in our endless rationality, on and on. We know everything, do we? You've never once had an experience, a feeling – of grandeur, bigger than yourself that makes you wonder whether there might be something that knows more than you do?

JOCASTA *backs away – stares at him.*

–

JOCASTA. You're a believer.

–

OEDIPUS. You're as blindly committed to your cause as they are to theirs, that I know.

JOCASTA. A woman killed her child hoping for rain. There was no rain.

–

OEDIPUS. Whoever it was that witnessed Laius's murder and reported it to you, we get them back here now. We find the killers; the people are appeased, and we move.

THE PEOPLE *chant* OEDIPUS*'s name –* JOCASTA *and* OEDIPUS *can hear it.*

JOCASTA. They love you for it. That must feel nice.

What will you do when I die? Will you go chasing after Time? Or Death? Arrest it, hunt it down? Remove its teeth? What will you do then? How will you solve it?

CREON *enters.*

CREON. The people are waiting.

OEDIPUS. Yep.

CREON. They want names.

OEDIPUS. –

CREON. When you called on the Gods to answer the riddle of the Sphinx, the answer came through you. I find I can hear the voice of the Gods most clearly in solitude. Shall we pray together?

JOCASTA *stares at* OEDIPUS. OEDIPUS *looks uncomfortable*.

JOCASTA. You've got to double down now.

OEDIPUS. Jocasta says that there was a witness to the attack.

JOCASTA. Not Jocasta says, there was a witness, his servant, not everything is up for grabs.

OEDIPUS. We need information. Where was Laius killed? Was the carriage found, had anything been stolen? Were people questioned at the time? Did anyone record those interrogations?

CREON. If it's further guidance you are seeking, you could call on the great prophet, Tiresias.

JOCASTA (*laughs*). Bring in a raving hermit, that'll do it.

–

OEDIPUS. Get hold of Laius's servant.

JOCASTA. He's retired. He's a shepherd now.

OEDIPUS. Get him and if Tiresias will speak to us, and the people want to hear it, get her.

OEDIPUS *leaves*.

–

CREON. My family and I, just this morning, were saying how much we miss you.

JOCASTA. 'My family and I' – I know their names, Creon.

CREON. We miss your piety. We fear for your children.

Pause – JOCASTA *astonished*.

JOCASTA. You fear for my children?

CREON. Your loss won't have been in vain. The Gods have a plan.

JOCASTA. Laius was killed by robbers. The Oracle was wrong, Creon, we both know that.

CREON, *strangely calm, smiles at* JOCASTA.

CREON. You would find peace if you could find faith again.

JOCASTA. I don't need faith, I have love, real love of a real person, flesh, blood, flaws, I know him, and he knows me. There is truth – there is truth between us. If you warp him with your...

CREON *leaves*.

THE PEOPLE *chant* OEDIPUS*'s name*.

Dance

Scene Four

OEDIPUS *stands in front of* THE PEOPLE. CREON *stands at his side*.

From the back – TIRESIAS *is brought forward against her will*.

OEDIPUS. Great Tiresias.

TIRESIAS *is blind, and infinitely wise...*

CREON. God-inspired seer of the wise and hidden mysteries.

OEDIPUS. We have the utmost respect for you /

TIRESIAS. / Then why was I dragged here?

OEDIPUS. We are in search of those who killed /

TIRESIAS. / Say it normally, you sound like you're pretending.

–

OEDIPUS. Okay. Who killed King Laius?

TIRESIAS *takes her time*.

Is that a dramatic pause or are you stumped?

–

Do you know who killed him?

TIRESIAS. Your men dragged me out of my house. I was having a cup of tea.

OEDIPUS. We're in desperate need of your help.

TIRESIAS. Help is something people offer. If you demand it, it becomes something else, no?

OEDIPUS. Great prophet, forgive our urgency but people are dying.

TIRESIAS. People are always dying, it's their defining feature.

TIRESIAS *senses the lack of* JOCASTA.

Your wife isn't standing with you.

OEDIPUS. She's inside with our children.

TIRESIAS. Why? Pious family and she didn't want to meet the great prophet Tiresias?

OEDIPUS. Our children are suffering.

TIRESIAS. Did you just use your children's suffering as a cover for your wife's scepticism?

OEDIPUS *stares at her, as if he might be moved to anger.*
OEDIPUS *whispers to* CREON. CREON *exits.*

OEDIPUS (*kneels*). I promise you; you have our devotion. My family and I are people of the Gods.

TIRESIAS. Get up, boy. You don't know which way the wind is blowing.

OEDIPUS *turns to the crowd, recruits* THE PEOPLE.

OEDIPUS. Great Tiresias, we have spoken with the Gods, and we understand that if we find King Laius's murderers, the rains will come, and the people will be healed.

THE PEOPLE *celebrate*. CREON *returns with* ANTIGONE *who is carrying a cup of water.* OEDIPUS *guides her forward.* ANTIGONE *carries the small and precious cup of water to* TIRESIAS.

TIRESIAS. Water.

THE PEOPLE *react.* ANTIGONE *offers the water to* TIRESIAS. TIRESIAS *touches it.* ANTIGONE, *desperately thirsty, doesn't want to hand it over.*

OEDIPUS. Antigone, give the water to Tiresias as a sign of our thanks.

ANTIGONE *nods, tries to give it over. As* TIRESIAS *takes it,* ANTIGONE *pulls it back.*

Antigone.

TIRESIAS (*gives the cup back to* ANTIGONE). Drink, child, your need is greater than mine.

TIRESIAS *puts her hand on* ANTIGONE*'s head.* OEDIPUS *lurches forward, pulls* ANTIGONE *to him.*

Hm. What harm can I do, if I'm only make-believe?

OEDIPUS. No one here thinks you're /

TIRESIAS. / I can tell you the answer to your question, but you might not want to hear it.

OEDIPUS. I'm not sure we have time for riddles.

TIRESIAS. If you sat quietly, and listened, if you could bear the silence for long enough, you would realise that the answer that you seek is within you. By forcing it out of me, it will take you twice as long to believe it. So, if anyone is wasting time, King Oedipus /

/ OEDIPUS *forces* TIRESIAS *onto the microphone.* TIRESIAS *resists.*

CREON. Please.

OEDIPUS. Speak.

OEDIPUS *forcibly insists*.

Anyone who withholds information is committing a crime. I've been quite clear.

TIRESIAS. You want to know who killed King Laius?... You killed King Laius.

Tiny beat. OEDIPUS *laughs*.

King Oedipus killed King Laius.

OEDIPUS. Okay, very good. And what evidence does the prophet have for her claim? Let's hear it.

TIRESIAS. I don't do evidence.

OEDIPUS. Of course you don't. Who does? Hey. If you've got a hunch, you've got a hunch. We should respect that. You can leave. Go finish your cup of tea.

TIRESIAS *doesn't move*.

TIRESIAS. If this city wishes to be free of suffering, the People of Thebes must banish King Oedipus. He is the polluter of this land.

OEDIPUS. I think we're done with this, Creon. Thanks.

CREON. The prophet has spoken.

OEDIPUS. Excuse me?

TIRESIAS. It's the truth, and you dragged me here and forced me to speak it.

OEDIPUS. Listen, you don't get to just go around accusing people in power because you don't like how we treated you; you pluck a name out of the air? You're not embarrassed by how petty and transparent that is?

TIRESIAS. I answered your question.

OEDIPUS. The Oracle said – 'his murderer*s* were never punished' – 'the perpetrator*s*' – plural, and now she's saying there's only one man and that man is me? I didn't kill King Laius. If you want to listen to the Gods, listen to them – the Oracle said *perpetrators*. There is a *factual inconsistency*. Are you listening?

OEDIPUS *looks out to* THE PEOPLE.

TIRESIAS. They don't seem to be. It sounds a little petty and transparent to me.

OEDIPUS. Are you seriously trying to condemn a man on the back of a 'prophecy'?

CREON. You were willing to do the same minutes ago. What greater nobility is there than to stand by your own word even when it's you that suffers from it?

OEDIPUS. Is this a coup?

CREON. I have all the benefits of royal association with none of the responsibility. Why would I want to be King?

OEDIPUS *looks at* THE PEOPLE.

OEDIPUS. Imprison Tiresias. Put Creon beyond the city gates before nightfall!

TIRESIAS (*with huge power*). Not only did you kill King Laius, but you have engaged, in the most shameful way, with those closest to you. A terrible curse will drive you from this land into darkness; a darkness so deep that when you cry out, no one will hear you. You will be unpicked from the fabric of your own society. You will be cast out and take your wife and children down with you. You will become blind where you had sight, you will become a beggar where you had wealth. To your children, you will become a brother as well as a father, to your wife you will become son as well as husband.

–

THE PEOPLE *are baying for blood, the banishment/ destruction of* OEDIPUS *becomes key to their salvation.*

OEDIPUS *exits into the Palace.*

CREON *faces the crowd. He raises his hands, channels divinity – he thrums with the power of it.*

Dance

Scene Five

JOCASTA *stands inside the Palace* – OEDIPUS *enters*.

–

JOCASTA. We should leave, just us. Our family.

OEDIPUS. You should have been out there with me.

JOCASTA. Did you hear me?

OEDIPUS. They can't depose me. They can't banish a king without proof.

JOCASTA. They have proof – it's just not a proof that we endorse. There will be no convincing them.

OEDIPUS. The shepherd, is he on his way? He'll testify. He'll say it wasn't me.

JOCASTA. It won't stand against Tiresias.

OEDIPUS. It's an eye-witness account versus a blind lady that wasn't at the scene.

JOCASTA. That's what you decided to meddle in.

OEDIPUS. Okay, so I play them at their own game. Give them someone easier to hate than me. Who do they want dead?

JOCASTA. More than the King? I think everyone wants the King dead a little bit, don't they?

OEDIPUS. So, help me, Jocasta – help me! Because all I've been doing is trying to keep everyone alive!

JOCASTA. Once you consult an Oracle, there is no way back. We have to go.

OEDIPUS. There is a way. There has to be. I'll solve it.

JOCASTA. I had a child with Laius… when we were married… A baby boy. As soon as Laius saw our child, he felt certain that he was going to die. He couldn't sleep. He couldn't eat. He was terrified. He couldn't stop picturing his own death. Creon advised him to consult with the Oracle. The Oracle said that my child would – the Oracle told Laius that he would die at the hands of his own offspring. But Laius wasn't killed by his child. He was killed by robbers, so the Oracle was wrong.

OEDIPUS. You had a child with Laius?

JOCASTA. You see what the Oracle does, it takes people's worst fears and instead of challenging the fear, it offers a solution. The more drastic and unthinkable the solution, the more it has silently, falsely confirmed the fear as real.

OEDIPUS. Where's the child now?

JOCASTA. Laius was convinced that the only way to save himself was to kill the baby. The child… my child, had his feet bound and was left by a servant, on a mountaintop, left to die. My tiny, perfect, child will have cried and cried – until he … – and I wasn't allowed to help him.

I was seventeen, Laius was a king. He told me to do it, I had no choice. You wonder why I didn't hunt his killer. I wasn't sure I really cared that he was dead. So you see that is the kind of thing that Oracles make people do. They have grown men killing babies, to make themselves feel safe. If an Oracle can make them kill a baby, you think they'll be dissuaded from killing you?

OEDIPUS. You had a baby?

A knock at the door – something different – someone has arrived.

CREON. There's a man asking to speak with the King.

OEDIPUS. If it's the shepherd, he'll report who murdered Laius. Let's hear him.

The CORINTHIAN *enters.*

JOCASTA. This isn't who I called for.

The CORINTHIAN *bows deeply in the presence of* OEDIPUS *and* JOCASTA.

CORINTHIAN. King Oedipus, Queen Jocasta, I'm honoured to be in your presence.

OEDIPUS. Who are you? Sorry, I – we don't know who you are.

CORINTHIAN. I'm a messenger from Corinth, your hometown, King Oedipus. I am a servant of the royal household. I come with good and bad news.

JOCASTA (*seeing the garlands*). There are flowers in Corinth?

OEDIPUS. What's the message?

CORINTHIAN. It concerns your parents. Queen Merope and King Polybus /

CREON. / There's no time for this. King Oedipus must be banished.

OEDIPUS. What's the message?

CORINTHIAN. King Oedipus of Thebes, is now, also, King Oedipus of Corinth.

Beat.

OEDIPUS. No. I'm Prince of Corinth. My father, King Polybus, is King of Corinth.

CORINTHIAN. King Polybus has died. All hail King Oedipus of Thebes and Corinth. Twice King.

The CORINTHIAN *places a garland around* OEDIPUS*'s neck with joy and pride.* OEDIPUS *looks at the flowers, smells them.* JOCASTA, *the* CORINTHIAN *and* CREON *watch him.*

CREON. The prophet Tiresias has declared this man the killer of King Laius. The salvation of the people relies /

JOCASTA. / Give him a minute; he's just lost his father.

CREON. And gained a kingdom.

JOCASTA. Give him a minute.

OEDIPUS. How did my father die?

CORINTHIAN. Peacefully, in his sleep.

–

OEDIPUS. I had things there were things I needed to, wanted to – I was going to see him and… but I can't do that now.

CORINTHIAN. The Corinthian people long to see their King.

JOCASTA. Does Corinth have water?

CORINTHIAN. Yes. It thrives.

CREON. The people are waiting.

OEDIPUS's words slowly build as he rounds on CREON until he's spitting with rage.

OEDIPUS. Uh-huh. Okay. Uh-huh. Um, you see, Creon – when I was a teenager, in Corinth, before I came here, I was in a bar one night… (*Clears his throat.*) and this guy, big guy – he's standing with this woman and he's looking at me and he's laughing, not a nice laugh and… I ask him why he's laughing, and he says, 'You're not the real Prince of Corinth and everyone knows it except for you'. Everyone in the bar looks away, pissy little snickering. I leave, I go home, I ask my parents about it – they say that that's just the kind of gossip people spread about a prince, and so I go back to the bar and I – find the woman that the guy was with. I knew, even though she was laughing with him, she was excited by being near a prince – she was working a little too hard to remain unaffected, that's the tell. I fucked her, out the back of the bar – then she called me a prince – and I walked out into the desert. I walked further and further, I was a teenage boy, I was confused and uncertain and – I had gone in search of, I had found, an Oracle. And that Oracle told me that I would sleep with my mother, and I would kill my father. And for a teenage boy, a young man, who, occasionally felt not right… who felt – I know, teenagers hey? – but hideous, here it was, explained by a mysterious… is that the kind of – at that age… to spend your life with that sort of, swimming around in your body, in your mind… and here we are, Creon – here we are, that in fact, my father just died, and I had nothing to do with it. Did you hear me?

CREON. This doesn't change anything.

OEDIPUS. It changes everything! My father died, and I had nothing to do with it. So, the Oracle was wrong. So, would you, and your priests and your *Gods* like to take account for the fact, take some fucking responsibility for the fact that my children never met their grandfather? That my father spent his life, without his son... just died without his son, just – that I have things to tell him, things to say, to tell him I love him, to show him my kids and my wife and – my dad, my dad – I'm never gonna see my dad again – you, you fuckers – because, because of the insipid, snake-charming, shit that you people... You disgust me.

What you did to her! What you and King Laius made her do! She was seventeen!

CREON. Your banishment will save the city. The people need /

OEDIPUS *goes for him;* CREON *tries to defend himself.* OEDIPUS *tries to calm down.*

OEDIPUS. The people need to rely on their own minds to make a decision. The people need to listen and access as much information as they can. The people need to struggle with nuance and difficulty, they need to come to hard and partial and practicable solutions. That's what they need to do.

CREON. They want you punished.

JOCASTA. Let's go to Corinth. We have two children. Will we make the journey?

CREON. You can't flee to Corinth; they won't allow it.

CORINTHIAN. He has a coronation to attend.

JOCASTA. Oedipus, we're going. There are flowers growing in Corinth.

–

OEDIPUS. Not yet. I won't go to Corinth. Not yet.

CREON. Why?

–

JOCASTA. You think these people still deserve you as a king?

CREON. It's not that.

OEDIPUS. I can't go to Corinth; I can't... I can't go – it's – if Queen Merope lives, I won't go to Corinth.

CREON. Because you fear the word of the Oracle.

Beat.

JOCASTA. Oedipus.

OEDIPUS (*to* CREON). Do you see what you people do?

–

CORINTHIAN. Forgive me for smiling but you don't have anything to fear. You can come to Corinth and see your mother because, Queen Merope and King Polybus, they loved you as if you were their own, but... they – they couldn't have children. So, after many years of trying, you were found and given to them, considered a gift from the Gods. He wasn't your father – she wasn't your mother. So, as far as what the Oracle decreed, you have nothing to fear from Queen Merope. You had nothing to fear from King Polybus. You can return home. The Queen will be so happy, and so will all of Corinth. There will be dancing in the streets.

–

JOCASTA *reaches for* OEDIPUS. *He steps away.* CREON *stands.*

–

OEDIPUS. Who told you that my parents were not my parents?

CORINTHIAN. No one told me. I was the servant who gave you to them when you were a baby.

OEDIPUS. Gave them... from where? Are you my father?

CORINTHIAN. No.

OEDIPUS. Who...

Pause – OEDIPUS *stares.*

CORINTHIAN. You were handed to me by a stranger. He said nothing, then asked me if I could offer the child a good life, I said yes, then he made me swear to care for the baby, I did – and that made him happy. He handed you to me – and he left.

Pause.

I have watched you – I have watched your progress with such pride.

OEDIPUS, *turns to* JOCASTA, *almost possessed with hope.*

OEDIPUS. The Oracle prophesied terrible things, and I believed them – that feeling. But there was nothing wrong with me – just that my mother was poor, or in trouble, or – those who left me, and those who raised me, so much love. That's it, that's all. That's the mystery. The shepherd will arrive. He will testify that King Laius was killed by robbers. He will testify that I am not the murderer that Creon and that mob seek. So now, I, as King of Thebes and King of Corinth – can lead our people, Theban people, to Corinth. This is how it was meant to be; I will unite my home cities – I will lead us all to salvation. We will thrive.

Dance

Scene Six

The SHEPHERD/SERVANT *enters. He's nervous.*

The CORINTHIAN *recognises the* SHEPHERD. *The* SHEPHERD *does not recognise the* CORINTHIAN.

–

JOCASTA *feels deeply at seeing the* SHEPHERD.

–

JOCASTA. This is the shepherd I sent for, King Laius's servant. He will confirm that Laius was killed by robbers, and we will be free to go to Corinth.

SHEPHERD. My Queen.

They greet each other with great fondness.

JOCASTA. It's good to see you.

SHEPHERD. You've got two girls now?

JOCASTA. A joy.

SHEPHERD. I'm sure.

JOCASTA (*turning to* THE PEOPLE). This man witnessed the murder of King Laius. He survived the attack. He came back and reported the events of Laius's death to me. Tell the people what you saw.

–

The SHEPHERD *looks about. The* SHEPHERD *stares at* OEDIPUS – *denial rages in him*.

–

SHEPHERD. Yes. I was a servant in the royal household. We were travelling in the desert. King Laius wanted to revisit the Oracle –

Beat. The SHEPHERD *looks about, he smiles at* JOCASTA.

– then there were men, robbers, desert people – five or six of them, appeared from nowhere. Angry, carrying clubs – demanding water, money – anything.

JOCASTA (*to the* SHEPHERD). Was King Oedipus one of those men?

They stare at one another.

CREON (*to* THE PEOPLE). How can we take the word of a retired servant, over and above the word of the prophet Tiresias? This man has been loyal to you for years. Deeply loyal, you leant on him in times of trouble.

OEDIPUS. Let him speak.

JOCASTA glares at CREON.

CREON. It makes good sense that he'd lie to try and protect your family now.

OEDIPUS. Are you a religious man?

The SHEPHERD nods.

SHEPHERD. Yes.

OEDIPUS. Swear on the Gods that you never saw my face before I came here to Thebes and was crowned King.

CREON. Swear.

SHEPHERD. I swear, I swear that I –

CORINTHIAN. My friend, you are going to perjure yourself without realising it, he – I can't witness – I can't let him do that before the Gods.

The SHEPHERD stares at the CORINTHIAN.

SHEPHERD. Who are you?

CORINTHIAN. You don't recognise me, but I remember you well. You have seen Oedipus's face before. I was there when you saw each other.

OEDIPUS. When?

SHEPHERD. How can you have been?

CORINTHIAN. It's alright – I've already told them the truth.

SHEPHERD. Why?

CREON. Speak the truth.

THE PEOPLE *echo: 'Speak! Speak!'*

SHEPHERD (*to* JOCASTA). You had suffered so much.

JOCASTA. What do you mean?

SHEPHERD. The day that King Oedipus arrived in Thebes… the day after the death of King Laius, there was *so much joy*.

King Oedipus answered the Sphinx, the rains came – and when you came out to greet this stranger, this young man, he walked towards you, across the sand, in the rain – when you saw him, you were filled with a joy that I hadn't seen in you since... when you looked at each other for the first time, I've never seen such...

JOCASTA. Love.

SHEPHERD. Joy, life – you smiled at each other and *such* a feeling of life.

CORINTHIAN. That wasn't the first time you'd seen him.

SHEPHERD (*breaks down*). I know, I know – but... it was so stupid. King Laius was always so... A fight about getting out of the road, neither man would move, both stubborn, there was miles of desert either side, heaven knows why, there was nothing to it, a squabble, and then before you knew it, he started – to try and defend himself and – I don't know if he had any idea he'd done it. He ran and... by the time I got back to the city, he was here, and he'd solved the Sphinx, the rains had come, the people adored him, Jocasta was happy – and I thought if I was the only one that knew, then... what did it matter? Everything was better because he'd arrived.

OEDIPUS. Where was King Laius killed?

SHEPHERD. In the place where the three roads meet.

TIRESIAS *appears, she stands with the* SHEPHERD *and the* CORINTHIAN.

OEDIPUS *sits with his face in his hands.*

OEDIPUS. After that night in the bar, after consulting the Oracle... I'd forgotten, there was a man, in the desert, that blocked my path –

JOCASTA. What do you mean blocked your path? It's the desert, there's nothing but space.

OEDIPUS. I was so angry about what the Oracle had said, so full of this terrible feeling – when this guy, in his big carriage, starts shouting at me, and I'm so clearly hungry and thirsty and he tells me to move – and – one of his men comes at me, tries to speak to me and – I push him aside, I go for the guy that's shouting at me, he's shouting like I'm nothing, like I'm some hideous – I'm so angry, I – just keep on and on... I run straight after, I run – but I... I beat him, badly. Maybe I – maybe I beat him badly enough that he – I was so angry, blind with /

SHEPHERD. / Who wants to hear, on a day of such celebration, that their new hope is also the man that caused the death of the old King?

JOCASTA. No.

SHEPHERD. You were so happy, when you saw him.

CREON. You let her marry her husband's murderer.

SHEPHERD. I did it for joy. (*To* OEDIPUS.) I don't think you had any idea it was King Laius. We were travelling without any signs of royalty, for protection. So it was just an enraged old man who spoke to you as if you were nothing. The boy deserves compassion not punishment.

TIRESIAS. King Oedipus killed King Laius.

CREON. King Oedipus killed King Laius. He is the polluter of this land.

JOCASTA (*to the* CORINTHIAN). You knew this, and you didn't say?

CORINTHIAN. No. I knew nothing about the death of King Laius. These men have met twice then – once on that awful day in the desert, but years before as well on a much happier day.

JOCASTA/SHEPHERD. When?

CORINTHIAN. When Oedipus was small and smiling and perfect and innocent. This was the child that you handed to me, with his feet bound, on Mount Cithaeron, you asked me if I could give him a good life. You tasked me to love him. Look, an unknown lowly child, has been well loved, loved excellently, and become twice King. A child born of such humble beginnings – has had the best of lives. A miracle, divine providence – surely?

JOCASTA *and* CREON *back off in shock.*

SHEPHERD. No.

OEDIPUS *goes forward, towards the* SHEPHERD.

OEDIPUS. Are you my father? Are you who left me? Who was my mother?

JOCASTA. No.

OEDIPUS. What's wrong? You're horrified you married a shepherd boy by mistake?

JOCASTA. No.

CREON. Horror.

OEDIPUS. You're my father.

SHEPHERD. No.

TIRESIAS. Who fathered this child, shepherd, if it wasn't you?

The SHEPHERD *breaks down.*

JOCASTA. They told you to leave him on the mountain. You came back and said the child had died. You told me my baby boy had died.

CORINTHIAN (*to* JOCASTA). Your child?

SHEPHERD. Who can leave a child to die, a baby? For love, no one can do that, for love.

CREON. An abomination.

JOCASTA. My child –

OEDIPUS *stares at* JOCASTA.

–

TIRESIAS (*as if it was a plain and simple fact*). Not only did you kill King Laius, but you have engaged, in the most shameful way, with those closest to you. A terrible curse will drive you from this land into darkness; a darkness so deep that when you cry out, no one will hear you. You will be unpicked from the fabric of your own society. You will be cast out and take your wife and children down with you. You will become blind where you had sight, you will become a beggar where you had wealth. To your children, you will become a brother as well as a father, to your wife you will become son as well as husband.

OEDIPUS. Exactly as the Oracle prophesied.

Dance

Scene Seven

OEDIPUS *and* JOCASTA – TIRESIAS *remains*.

OEDIPUS *tries to leave*.

–

JOCASTA. No. No – there's a world where we can… we can go – there are flowers in Corinth…

As mother and son – family – we can lead the people to safety.

How can we be punished for a crime we didn't know we were committing?

–

OEDIPUS. I am banished. The rains will come, and the people will be healed.

JOCASTA. We don't know that.

OEDIPUS. We don't know?

OEDIPUS *walks away from* JOCASTA.

JOCASTA. Our girls, I...

–

If Laius hadn't given into his fear, if we'd kept you, if you'd stayed with Merope and Polybus – if – if – Laius had let you pass – if – you hadn't consulted – it wasn't a given, none of it was a given, it's fear, it's always fear, every time... I said, I told you – fear makes it happen; it drives it – don't let it, fight – the... I can't lose my child again.

OEDIPUS *exits*.

–

JOCASTA *hears the sound of rain*.

It's rain. It's just rain.

Dance *begins*.

ANTIGONE *and* ISMENE (*call from offstage*). Mama! Mama! It's raining! Look, the rain!

TIRESIAS. If you don't leave, they'll kill you.

JOCASTA. I can't leave my girls.

TIRESIAS. The girls will stay – they have more story to tell.

JOCASTA. I can't leave them.

ANTIGONE *and* ISMENE *call from offstage*.

ISMENE. Come, Mama. There's rain!

ANTIGONE. Come!

TIRESIAS. An absent mother is better than a dead mother.

JOCASTA. An absent mother can come back when the tides turn.

TIRESIAS. Maybe.

TIRESIAS *gives* JOCASTA *a bag*.

JOCASTA. You're a prophet, tell me if I see my children again.

TIRESIAS. You don't believe in prophets.

JOCASTA. Look after my girls.

TIRESIAS. I will try.

> JOCASTA *escapes – she leaves Thebes never to return.*
>
> CREON *enters.*

CREON. Where's Jocasta?

TIRESIAS. Gone.

CREON. Gone where? The Gods must hear her repent and the people must see it.

TIRESIAS. Why? You have your rain.

CREON. She must be shamed.

> TIRESIAS *laughs.*

TIRESIAS. You won't catch her. I wouldn't bother trying.

CREON. She must be shamed!

> ***Dance*** *continues.*

> OEDIPUS *enters from the back – through the middle – with his eyes put out.*

Scene Eight

It's raining. OEDIPUS, *eye-less, presents himself at the front of the Palace.* CREON *and* THE PEOPLE *look on.*

OEDIPUS. Good Thebans, I am guilty, guilty of the pride and mindless rage that saw me kill King Laius... my father. I am guilty of the hubris that had me presume I solved the Sphinx with my own mind, when in fact the Gods were speaking through me. I am guilty of the cynicism with which I treated the word of the Oracle. I am guilty of refusing to believe Tiresias. I am guilty of every second that I have wasted, of every death that I have caused.

I thought I could seek and find the answer.

I have removed my arrogant eyes. Only the Gods can see. Darkness is the soil in which I nurture my humility.

My banishment, at last – (*He feels the rain.*) brings you salvation. Where's Jocasta?

CREON. She's gone.

THE PEOPLE *object.* CREON *steps forward.*

Be assured... be assured... having been forced to consider the weight of her sin, Jocasta ran through the Palace. She screamed with shame. She had already pulled some of her hair out. She locked herself in her marital bedroom. No one could get in. She shouted for Laius. She shouted for Oedipus. She shouted for the Gods, desperately begging for their forgiveness. She retched with disgust at having had children with her own child. We broke the door in and found her hanging in her own bedroom, from her own bedsheets.

OEDIPUS. Is it true?

CREON. She came to God, at last. She came to faith. Let us learn this lesson: there are forces, greater than ourselves, that we do not understand... forces that move us. The Gods must be feared, respected and obeyed or else great suffering will befall you. The stain on this family will be everlasting. Put King Oedipus beyond the city walls.

THE PEOPLE, *vindicated – redeemed – celebrate triumphantly.*

OEDIPUS *is led out of the city.*

THE PEOPLE *worship at the feet of* CREON, *their new King.*

Dance

Scene Nine

Outside the city walls.

OEDIPUS, *alone, stumbles in the darkness. The sun is starting to set. It's getting dark.*

ANTIGONE *appears.* ISMENE – *smaller, hangs back afraid.*

–

ANTIGONE. Are you okay?

OEDIPUS. Antigone?

ANTIGONE. It's me and Ismene. She doesn't want to come close.

OEDIPUS. Both of you, leave – you shouldn't be here. Go back to Uncle Creon.

–

OEDIPUS *walks on a little way. His daughters watch him.*

ISMENE *doesn't like it; she turns and runs – exits.*

Have you gone?

ANTIGONE *doesn't respond for a while.*

ANTIGONE. I'll help you.

OEDIPUS. Go back.

ANTIGONE. I'll help you.

OEDIPUS. You shouldn't have to.

ANTIGONE. Well then you shouldn't have taken your eyes out.

Long pause.

You looked after me a thousand times when I was small, it's fine. Come on.

ANTIGONE *helps her father.*

They stop.

OEDIPUS. Is there rain? I'm not sure I can still feel it. Is it still raining? Antigone?

ANTIGONE. The rain has stopped, for now. Maybe it will begin again.

OEDIPUS. What do you see? Antigone? Tell me. Are the people healed?

Curtain call.

Dance

www.nickhernbooks.co.uk

@nickhernbooks